CUB selfie

the self

/ Sɛlfi /

Learn how to pronounce

noun

INFORMAL

noun: **selfie** ; plural noun: **selfies** ; noun: **selfy**

1. a photograph that one has taken of
oneself, typically taken with a smartphone
or webcam and shared via social media.
"occasional selfies are acceptable, but
posting a new picture of yourself every day is
not necessary

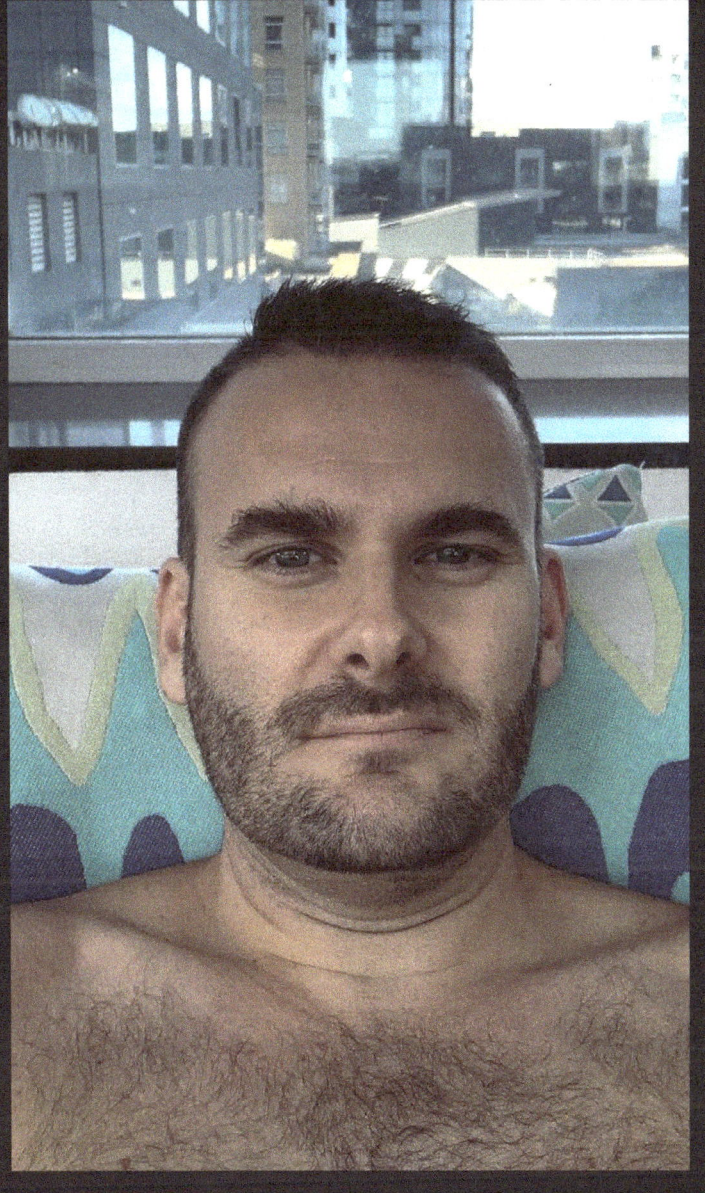

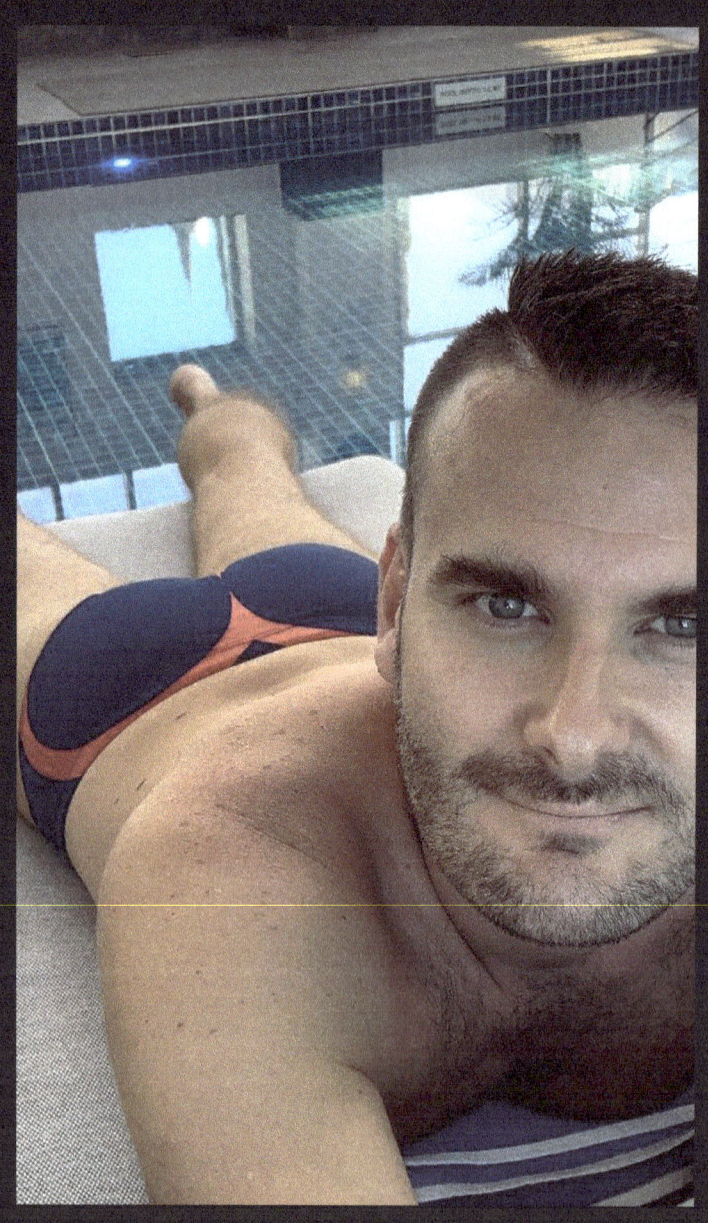

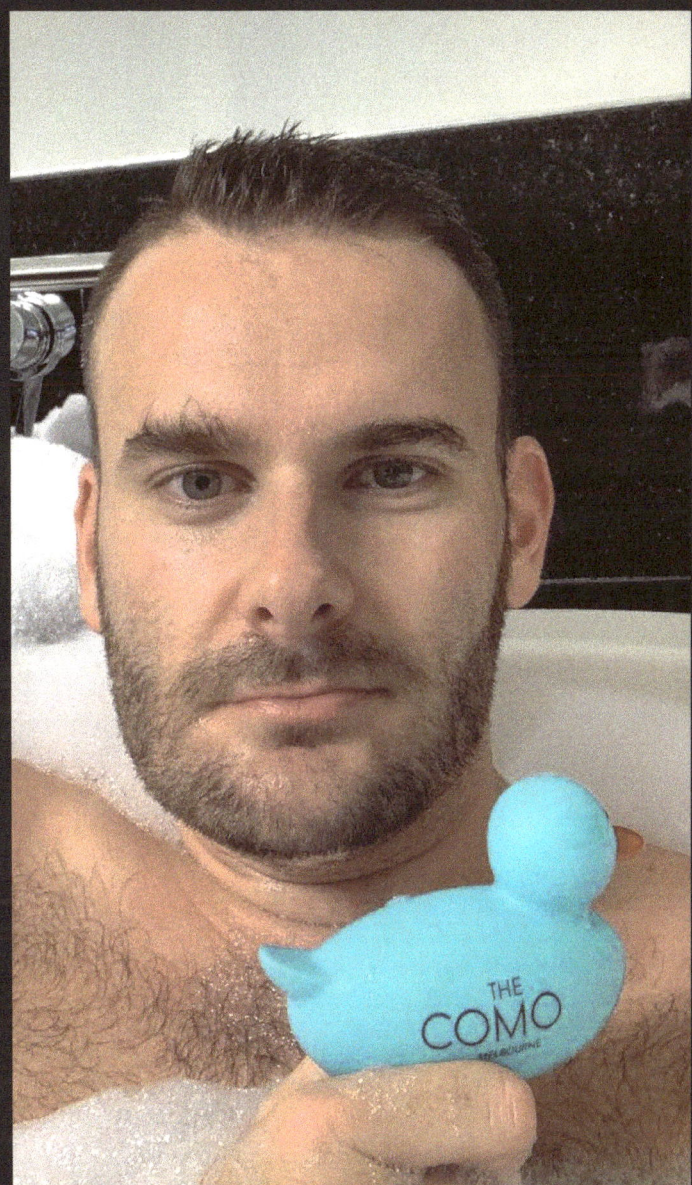

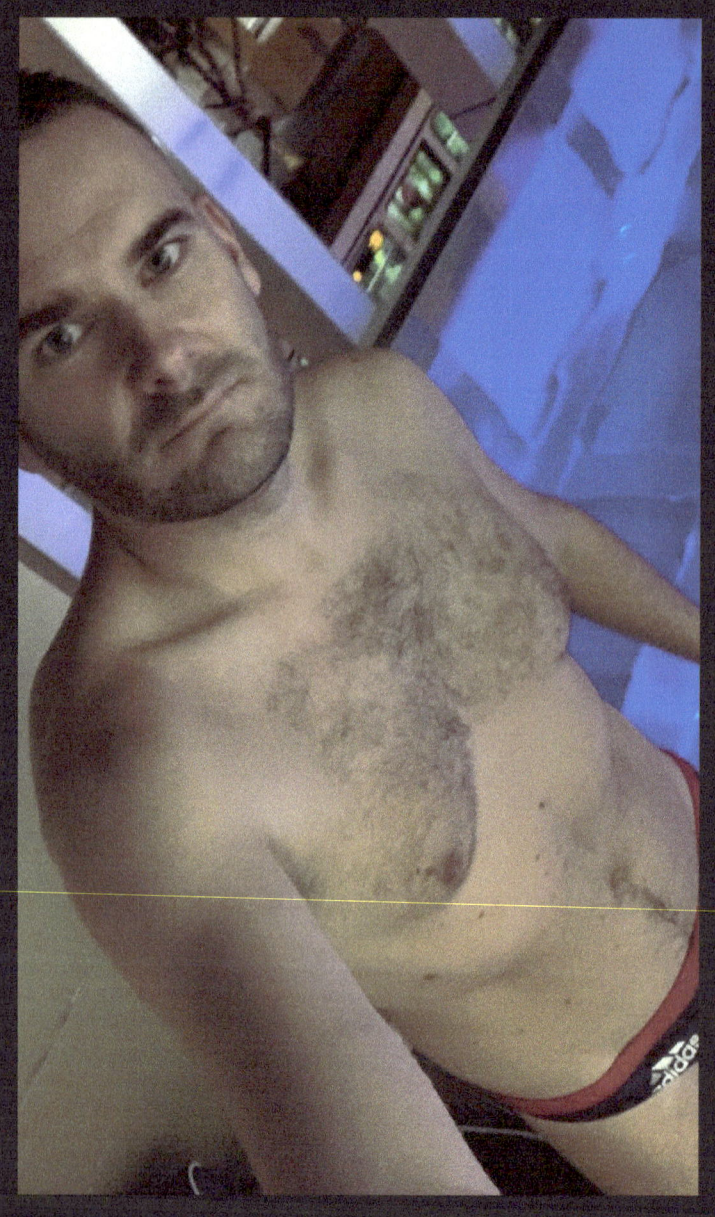

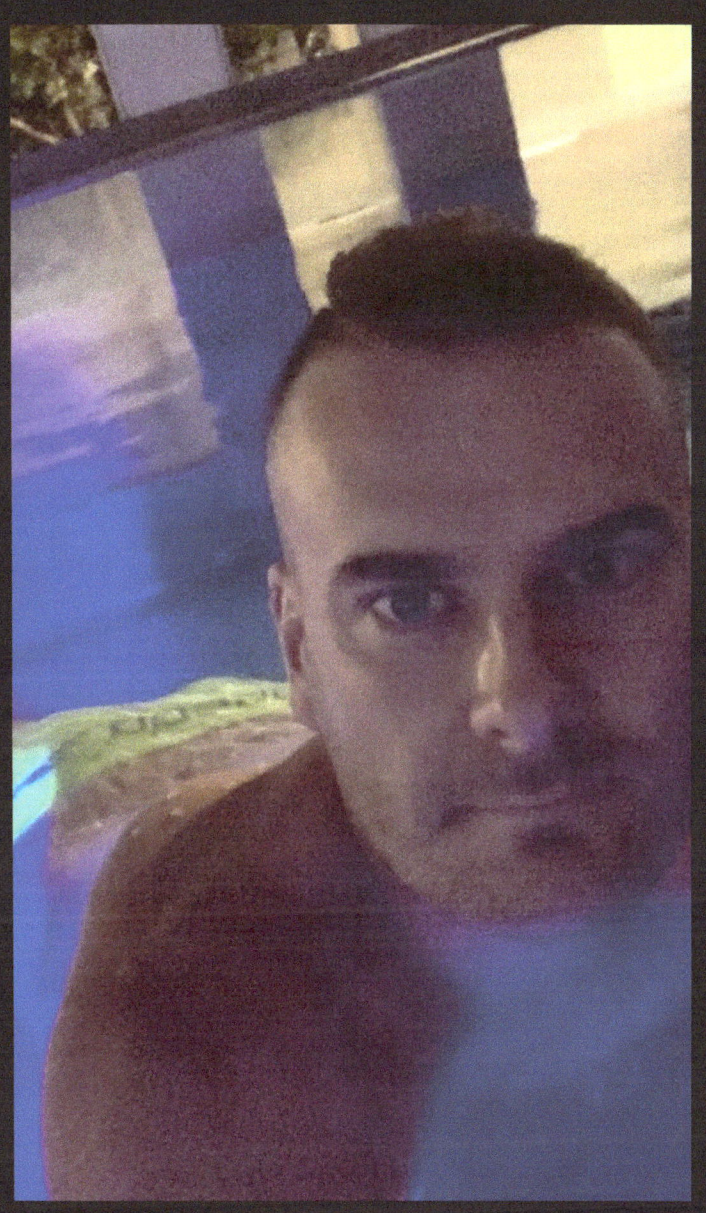

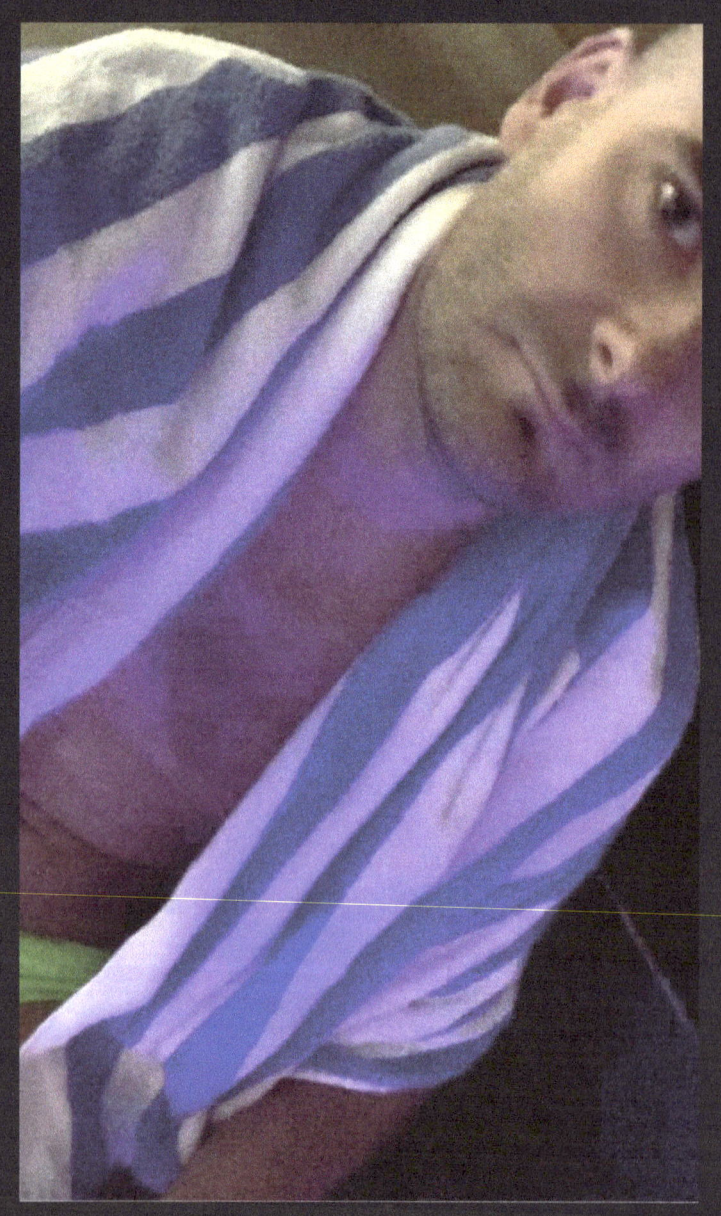

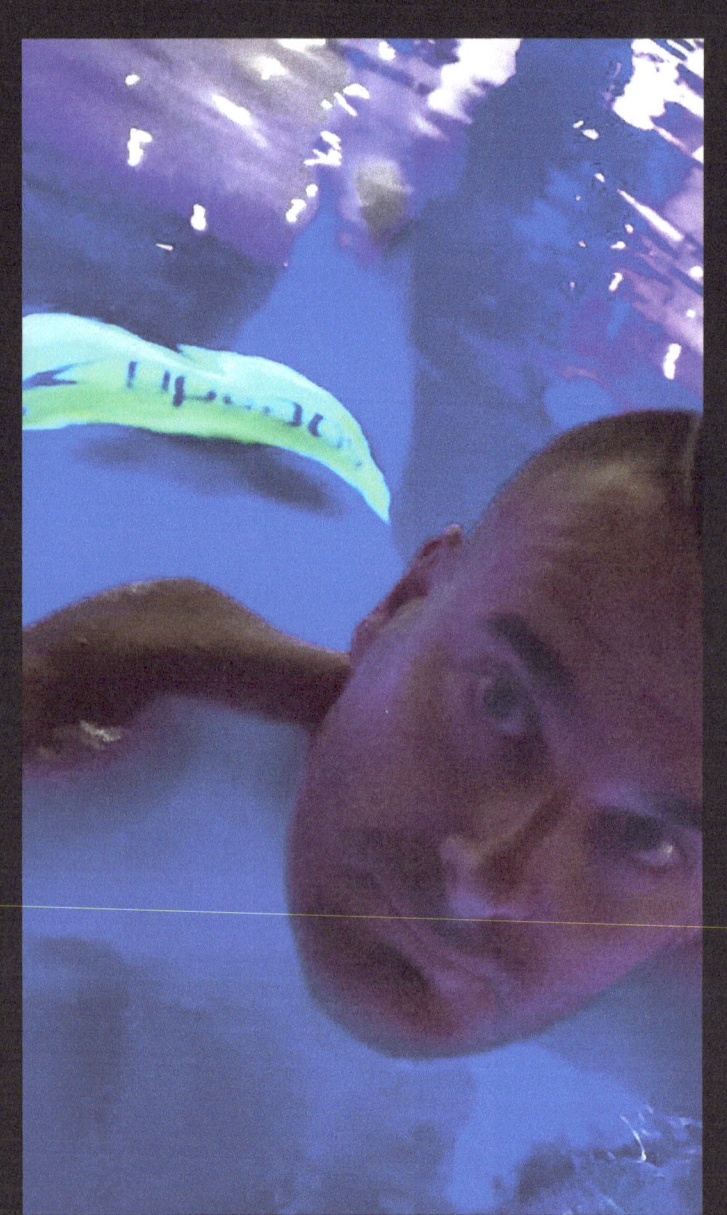

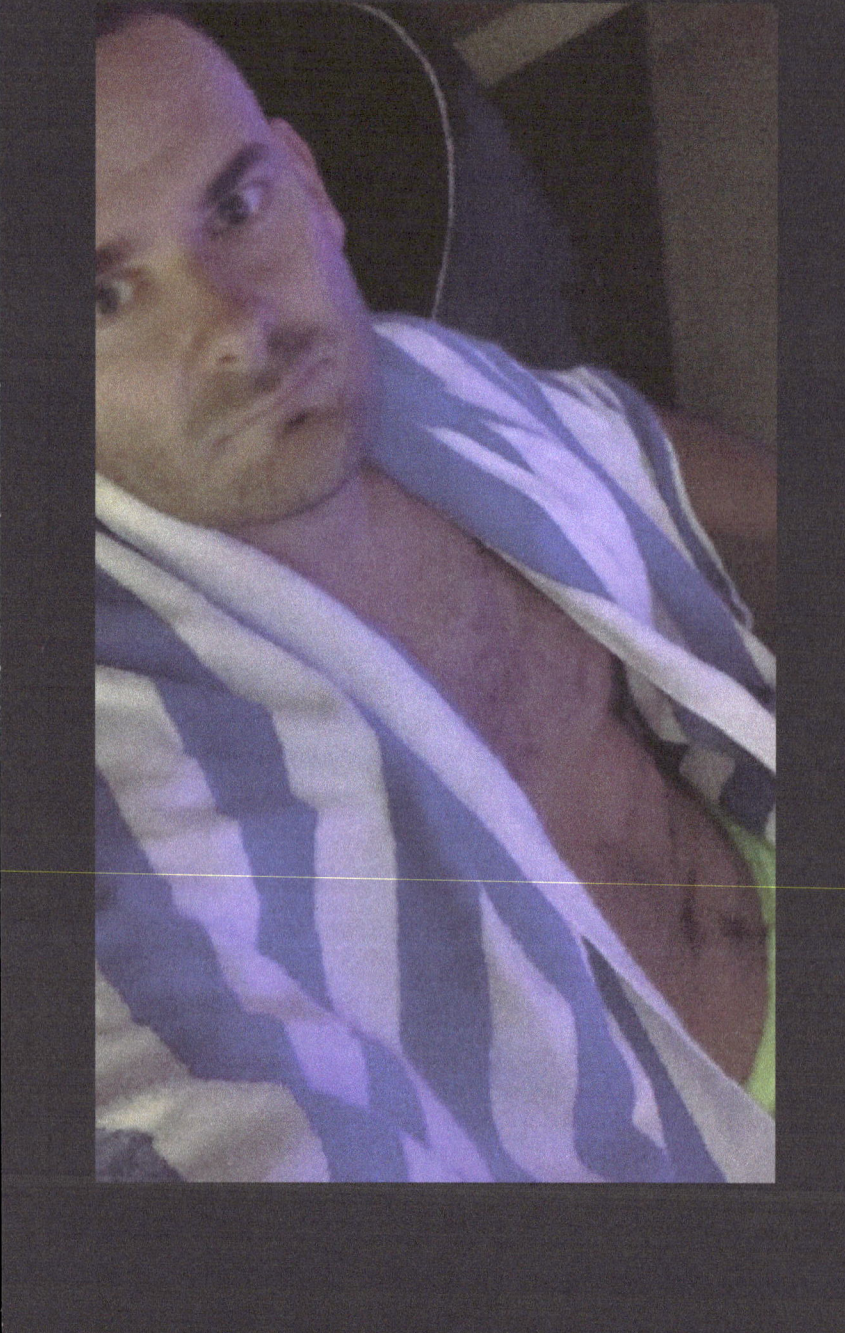

CPSIA information can be obtained
at www.ICGtesting.com
Printed in the USA
BVHW020535290619
552120BV00032B/482/P